MW01196924

This Sketchbook Belongs to:

____

____

Made in the USA
Las Vegas, NV
27 August 2023

76710767R00072